It's an Apple Tree!

¡Es un manzano!

Elisa Peters

Traducción al español:
Eduardo Alamán

PowerKiDS press™ & **Editorial Buenas Letras**™

New York

For Hannah Budnitz and Guy Williams, two accomplished fruit pickers

Published in 2009 by The Rosen Publishing Group, Inc.
29 East 21st Street, New York, NY 10010

First Edition

Editor: Amelie von Zumbusch
Book Design: Greg Tucker
Photo Researcher: Jessica Gerweck

Photo Credits: Cover, pp. 5, 7, 9, 11, 13, 15, 17, 19, 23, 24 by Shutterstock.com; p. 21 © www.istockphoto.com/Raoul Wernede.

Library of Congress Cataloging-in-Publication Data

Peters, Elisa.
  [It's an apple tree! Spanish & English]
  It's an apple tree! = ¡Es un manzano! / Elisa Peters ; traducción al español, Eduardo Alamán. – 1st ed.
      p. cm. – (Everyday wonders = Maravillas de todos los dias)
  Includes index.
  ISBN 978-1-4358-2522-2 (library binding)
  1. Apples–Juvenile literature. I. Title. II. Title: ¡Es un manzano!
  SB363.P3818 2009
  634'.11–dc22
                                        2007052992

Manufactured in the United States of America

Web Sites: Due to the changing nature of Internet links, PowerKids Press and Editorial Buenas Letras have developed an online list of Web sites related to the subject of this book. This site is updated regularly. Please use this link to access the list: www.powerkidslinks.com/wonder/apple/

Contents/Contenido

Do you like apples?

¿Te gustan las manzanas?

⑤

Apples grow on apple trees.

Las manzanas crecen en árboles llamados manzanos.

An **orchard** has many apple trees.

En un **manzanal** hay muchas manzanas.

9

Some apples are **green**.

Algunas manzanas
son **verdes**.

Many apples are **red**.

Muchas manzanas son **rojas**.

In the spring, apple trees are covered in **blossoms**.

En la primavera los manzanos se cubren de **flores**.

These blossoms will turn
into apples.

Estas flores se convertirán
en manzanas.

⑰

By fall, it is time to pick
the apples.

Las manzanas se cosechan
en el otoño.

19

Farmers pick apples and
send them to stores.

Los agricultores cosechan
las manzanas y las envían
a los mercados.

Picking apples is fun!

¡Cosechar manzanas es
muy divertido!

Words to Know/Palabras que debes saber

**blossoms
(las) flores**

**green
verde**

**orchard
(el) manzanal**

**red
rojo**

Index

Índice